FALL

Phonemic Awareness Songs & Rhymes

♪ Fun Lyrics Sung to Familiar Tunes 🎵

• Written by •

Kimberly Jordano & Trisha Callella-Jones

Editor: Kristine Johnson

Illustrator: Darcy Tom

Project Director: Carolea Williams

Table of Contents

Introduction

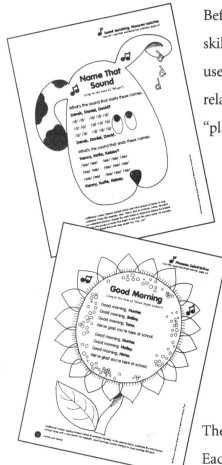

Before children learn to read words in print, they must develop the important skill of auditory discrimination—an awareness of how letters and words are used in oral language. *Phonemic Awareness Songs & Rhymes* provides theme-related songs and activities that encourage children to manipulate sounds and "play with language." Children learn to

- *listen for and identify rhyming words.*
- *identify words that include the same sound.*
- *listen for and count syllables within a word.*
- *identify the beginning, middle, and ending sounds in words.*
- *count and clap out the number of sounds in words.*
- *combine letter sounds to form words.*
- *divide words into separate sounds.*
- *match sounds to letters of the alphabet.*

The activities and songs in this resource are both easy to use and fun to do. Each reproducible activity card and song sheet clearly identifies the phonemic-awareness task(s) being reinforced. The cards and song sheets also indicate which songs and activities can be taught together. *Phonemic Awareness Songs & Ryhmes* also includes supplementary reproducibles and a helpful cross-check index to simplify lesson preparations. If you are unfamiliar with any of the tunes, simply chant the song as a rhyme. This is an all-in-one resource filled with fun, interactive activities and silly, playful songs—a winning combination for any reading-development program!

What Is Phonemic Awareness?

Phonemic awareness is the ability to recognize and manipulate individual sound units (phonemes) in spoken language: to examine language independent of meaning, to see relationships between sounds in words, and to rearrange sounds to create new words. For example, the word *chick* is made up of three phonemes (/ch/ /i/ /k/*); it can be changed to the word *pick* by replacing /ch/ with /p/.

Students who are phonemically aware are able to master the following tasks:

Rhyming—The ability to identify and form rhyming words.

Example: Do these words rhyme?

fun—fan	*no*
pig—wig	*yes*
cheer—year	*yes*
bread—seed	*no*

Sound Matching—The ability to hear and identify similar word patterns.

Example: Which word does not belong?

sun, sad, sip, tub	*tub*
mat, bat, hop, cat	*hop*
bee, meat, sea, fee	*meat*

* When letters appear between slash marks (such as /k/), the sound rather than the letter name is represented.

Syllable Counting—The ability to identify the number of syllables in spoken words.

Example: How many syllables do you hear in these words?

ticket	*2*
dog	*1*
bicycle	*3*
pencil	*2*

Syllable Splitting—The ability to identify onsets and rimes.*

Example: What word do you have when you join these sounds together?

j–ump	*jump*
t–an	*tan*
cl–imb	*climb*
str–eet	*street*

Phoneme Blending—The ability to orally blend individual sounds to form a word.

Example: What word do you have when you join these sounds together?

/m/ /a/ /p/	*map*
/j/ /a/ /k/	*jack*
/ch/ /ee/ /p/	*cheap*
/b/ /r/ /o/ /k/	*broke*

* An *onset* is all the sounds in a word that come before the first vowel. A *rime* is the first vowel in a word and all the sounds that follow. (For example, in the word *splash,* the onset is *spl-* and the rime is *-ash.*)

Phoneme Isolation—The ability to identify the beginning, middle, and ending sounds in a word.

Examples:

What's the beginning sound in *toe?*	/t/
What's the middle sound in *big?*	/i/
What's the ending sound in *plane?*	/n/

Phoneme Counting—The ability to count the number of phonemes in a word.

Example: How many sounds do you hear in these words?

at	2
lake	3
paint	4
tent	4

Phoneme Segmentation—The ability to break apart a word into individual sounds.

Example: Which sounds do you hear in these words?

mud	/m/ /u/ /d/
play	/p/ /l/ /a/
strike	/s/ /t/ /r/ /i/ /k/

Phoneme Addition—The ability to add a beginning, middle, or ending sound to a word.

Examples:

$$p + lay = play$$
$$grew + m = groom$$

What word would you have if you added /b/ to the beginning of *low?*   blow

What word would you have if you added /r/ to the middle of *bed?*   bread

What word would you have if you added /s/ to the end of *how?*   house

Phoneme Deletion—The ability to omit the beginning, middle, or ending sound from a word.

Examples:

What word would you have if you took out the /f/ in *flake?*   lake

What word would you have if you took out the /l/ in *play?*   pay

What word would you have if you took out the /t/ in *meat?*   me

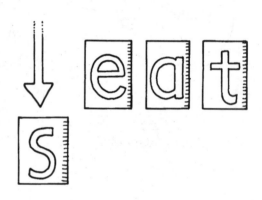

Phoneme Substitution—The ability to substitute a new sound for the beginning, middle, or ending sound of a word.

Examples:

What word would you have if you changed the /b/ in *ball* to a /t/?   tall

What word would you have if you changed the /o/ in *hot* to an /a/?   hat

What word would you have if you changed the /p/ in *map* to a /d/?   mad

Make the Most of It!

The songs and rhymes in this resource help lay a foundation for phonics instruction in a fun and exciting way. Use them when teaching specific phonemic-awareness tasks (see the song titles listed on individual activity cards), or follow the suggestions below to incorporate these "kid-captivating" songs and rhymes into your core curriculum.

Song Cards

Enlarge, decorate, and laminate each song for daily shared reading and singing. Use "magic wands" or theme-related reading sticks to point to the words as students sing the songs. Make a fun, accessible display by using clothespins to hang the song sheets from a plastic toy chain, or store the song sheets in baskets for use at a center or for free-choice reading time.

Individual Songbooks

Provide each student with a three-pronged folder. As a new song is learned, give each child a photocopy of the song sheet to decorate, read, sing, and then add to his or her notebook. Provide weekly opportunities for students to reread and sing their favorite songs. Send the notebooks home at Open House or at the end of the year for students to share with their families.

Songs on Tape

Practice singing the songs with your students. Once students are familiar with a song, use a tape recorder to make a class tape of the song. Place copies of the song sheets and the cassette at a listening center for students to use.

Favorite Colors

So many crayons in the box
   for you,
Red ones, yellow ones, blue
   ones, too.
But the one little crayon that
   rhymes with 〔bean〕
Is my favorite color.
It's the color _____.

Charts

Copy the songs onto large individual sheets of chart paper. Use different colored markers to write key words or sounds. Invite students to "frame" the key words with their hands or with Wikki Stix (available at teacher-supply stores), use a reading stick to point to the words, highlight key words with highlighters or highlighting tape (found at most office-supply stores), or cover words with sticky notes. For additional learning and fun, add to the chart related pictures or reproducible picture cards from the back of this resource.

Big Books

Write each line from one of the songs on a separate sheet of large construction paper. Invite students to draw pictures on the construction paper that correspond to each line. Bind pages into a class big book and display it in the class library for students to reread.

Photo Name Cards

Take a photograph of each child and of any classroom pets or puppets. Write each student's name on an index card, a sentence strip, or a tongue depressor, and then attach his or her photo to it. Place the photo name cards in a pocket chart or hold them up while you sing name-recognition songs.

Puppets

Make reduced copies of a song sheet, glue them to the backs of individual paper lunch sacks, and distribute them to students. Have students draw favorite song-related characters on the front of their sack to make paper-sack puppets. Invite the class to use the hand puppets while singing and dramatizing the corresponding song written on the back.

Flannel Board

Cover the song lyrics on the song sheet with paper, photocopy the song-sheet artwork onto card stock, and color the images. Photocopy any picture cards from the back of this resource that correspond to the song, cut them out, and color them. Invite students to draw pictures that correspond to the song, and then photocopy the pictures onto card stock. Glue felt or attach Velcro to the back of the card stock. Invite students to manipulate the images on a flannel board while singing the song.

Magnetic Board

Magnetic boards include cookie sheets, oven-burner covers, and magnetic chalkboards. Photocopy on card stock picture cards from the back of this resource, cut them out, and color them. Write song lyrics on sentence strips and alphabet letters on index cards. Add magnetic tape to the backs of the sentence strips, picture cards, and letter cards. Invite students to manipulate the images or letters on the magnetic board while singing the song.

Storyboards

Invite students to create a construction-paper backdrop that represents a scene from a song. Have students draw pictures, cut them out, and glue some of them directly on the backdrop to make a storyboard. Invite students to glue other pictures to craft sticks to be used as pointers or puppets while singing.

Music and Movement

March around the room with students while singing one of the songs. For extra fun, give students pom-poms and/or musical instruments to use while they sing. Ask a volunteer to "be the teacher" and point to each word on the song chart. Allow students to sing solos or duets in front of the class.

Themes and Topics

Enrich your studies by placing a copy of the song sheet on the back of theme-related projects, bulletin boards, illustrated wall stories, artwork, or class big books. Use the songs to introduce new units and to generate ideas for artwork.

Card Sorting

Place in a pocket chart picture cards from the back of this resource. Invite students to sort the picture cards by various categories, such as initial sound, final sound, rhyming pairs, number of sounds, or number of syllables. For additional learning, place the picture cards in a learning center for students to re-sort.

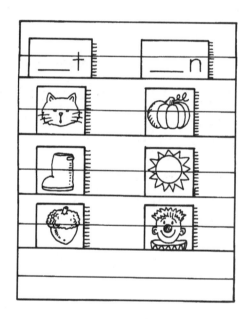

Rhyming March

Have students place their chairs in a circle. Place on the chairs picture cards from the back of this resource, and then have students march around the chairs while singing one of the songs. When the music stops, have students say a word that rhymes with the picture card next to them. Remind students that rhyming words can be nonsense words, too.

Reading Strategies

Write the lines of one of the songs on sentence strips and distribute them to different students. Also distribute any picture cards from the back of this resource if they correspond with the song. While singing the song, invite students to place their sentence strip or picture card in the appropriate place in the pocket chart. Prompt students with reading-strategy questions such as

What sound do you hear at the beginning of _____? What letter do you expect to see? Does that make sense, sound right, and look right? What would the first letter of the sentence look like? What do you expect to see at the end of the sentence? How many letters are in the word _____? How many words are in the sentence?

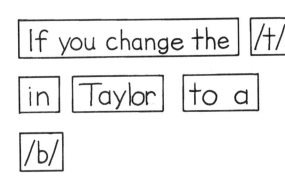

Sentence Manipulation

Write the lines of a song on sentence strips and then cut apart the strips into words or phrases. Write some consonants on index cards for students to substitute different phonemes. Invite students to rebuild or manipulate the song.

Jump Rope Chants

Invite students to jump rope or bounce a ball while chanting the songs. The steady beat of the jump rope will help children keep the rhyming pattern. Challenge students to continue jumping rope or bouncing the ball throughout an entire song.

Unscramble the Word

Print in large letters on a sentence strip a key word from one of the songs. Cut apart the letters, and pass out each letter to a different student. Invite students to bring their letter to the pocket chart and reassemble the word.

Be the Word

Write letters on separate index cards and distribute the cards to students. Call out a word from a song and invite students who have a letter from that word to stand in the correct order to "be," or rebuild, the

word. To "be" the sentence, write words from a song on separate index cards and pass them out. Have students stand in the correct order to rebuild the sentence.

Word Families

Use magnetic letters on a magnetic surface to spell a common rhyming word, such as *cat*. Invite students to replace the first letter of the word with another to form additional rhyming words, such as *bat*, *hat*, and *sat*. Extend learning by having students spell out high-frequency words used in the song lyrics.

Magic Reading Sticks

To make reading sticks for pointing to song lyrics while chanting or singing, have students dip the ends of chopsticks into brightly colored paint and sprinkle them with glitter. Invite students to tie ribbons to their "magical" reading stick. Create more reading sticks by using a hot glue gun to attach to dowels plastic animals or other small toys that correspond with subjects in the songs.

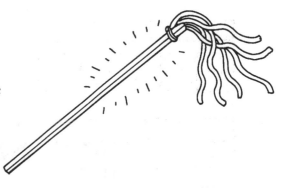

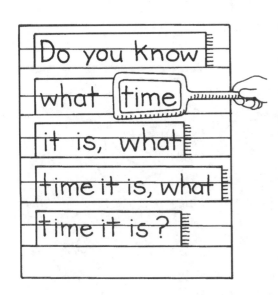

Word Hunts

Cut out a rectangular hole in the center of several brightly colored flyswatters so that when the flyswatters are placed over a word on a chart or a sentence strip, the word is framed. (Cut some holes longer than others so different-size words can be framed.) Invite a student to come to a chart or pocket chart and "hunt" for a word. For example, have a student hunt for a word that rhymes with *dime* and begins with /t/. The student then frames the word *time* using the flyswatter.

Magic Reading Glasses

Collect inexpensive plastic toy glasses (available at party-supply stores), and punch out the lenses. Add curling ribbon to the sides of each pair for a fun decoration. Place the glasses in a special place for students to wear while reading.

Very Special Visors

Collect a few plastic visors. Decorate the visors with puffy paint and glitter glue. Invite a "leader of the day" to wear the visor and choose a favorite song for the class to sing.

♫ Shake Hands ♫

(sing to the tune of "Looby Loo")

Shake hands with **Billy B**oo,
Shake hands with **Billy B**ay,
Shake hands with **Billy B**oo,
Let's sing it another way.

Stand up **Sandi S**oo,
Stand up **Sandi S**ay,
Stand up **Sandi S**oo,
Let's meet more friends that way.

Additional verses: Replace bolded names and letters to continue the song.
For example, *Shake hands with **Nancy N**oo.*

Fun with Names

(sing to the tune of "Alouette")

In the classroom,

Early in the morning

Hear the children

Playing with their sounds.

Change your name to start with **/t/**.

Change your name to start with **/t/**.

Name with **/t/**.

Name with **/t/**.

What's your name?

Shout it now. . . .

Note: Children shout out their altered name and then begin the next verse.

Additional verses: Replace bolded sounds to continue the song. For example, *Change your name to start with **/ch/**.*

Name That Sound

(sing to the tune of "Bingo")

What's the sound that starts these names:

Derek, Daniel, David?

/d/ /d/   /d/ /d/ /d/

/d/ /d/   /d/ /d/ /d/

/d/ /d/   /d/ /d/ /d/

Derek, Daniel, David.

What's the sound that ends these names:

Kenny, Katie, Kelsey?

/ee/ /ee/   /ee/ /ee/ /ee/

/ee/ /ee/   /ee/ /ee/ /ee/

/ee/ /ee/   /ee/ /ee/ /ee/

Kenny, Katie, Kelsey.

Additional verses: Replace bolded names with other groups of names to sing additional verses (for example, **Sam, Stuart, Sara** or **Amanda, Jenna, Hannah**). For additional practice, change the word *names* to *words* and replace the bolded names with groups of words that begin or end with the same sound. For example, *What's the sound that ends these words:* **toy, boy, joy?**

Fall Phonemic Awareness Songs & Rhymes © 1998 Creative Teaching Press

Singing Silly Names

(sing to the tune of "If You're Happy and You Know It")

If you change the **/k/** in **Kim** to a **/b/**,

If you change the **/k/** in **Kim** to a **/b/**,

If you change the **/k/** to **/b/**,

Then **Kim** turns into **Bim,**

If you change the **/k/** in **Kim** to a **/b/**.

Additional verses: Replace bolded sounds and names to continue the song.
For example, *If you change the **/d/** in **Dave** to a **/p/**.*

Good Morning

(sing to the tune of "Good Night Ladies")

Good morning, **Hunter.**

Good morning, **Bailey.**

Good morning, **Tana.**

We're glad you're here at school.

Good morning, **Nunter.**

Good morning, **Nailey.**

Good morning, **Nana.**

We're glad you're here at school.

Additional verses: Replace bolded names to continue the song. In the second stanza, substitute the initial sound of each name with a new sound. For example, *Good morning,* **Cooper** changes to *Good morning,* **Sh**ooper.

Fall Phonemic Awareness Songs & Rhymes © 1998 Creative Teaching Press

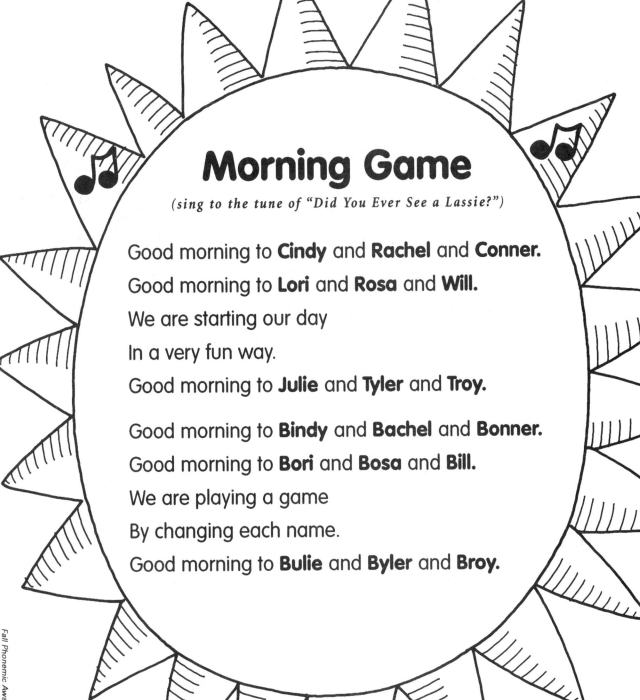

Morning Game

(sing to the tune of "Did You Ever See a Lassie?")

Good morning to **Cindy** and **Rachel** and **Conner**.

Good morning to **Lori** and **Rosa** and **Will**.

We are starting our day

In a very fun way.

Good morning to **Julie** and **Tyler** and **Troy**.

Good morning to **Bindy** and **Bachel** and **Bonner**.

Good morning to **Bori** and **Bosa** and **Bill**.

We are playing a game

By changing each name.

Good morning to **Bulie** and **Byler** and **Broy**.

Additional verses: Replace bolded names with other groups of names to sing additional verses. In the second stanza, substitute the initial sound of each name with a new sound. For example, *Good morning to* **Carrie** *and* **Justin** *and* **Nikki** changes to *Good morning to* **Tarrie** *and* **Tustin** *and* **Tikki**.

Name Game

Phoneme Substitution

Materials

- "Shake Hands" song (page 16)

- sentence strips

- pocket chart

- index cards

- student photos

- glue

- gift bag

Print on sentence strips the words to "Shake Hands" with bolded words omitted, and place the strips in a pocket chart. Write student names on index cards and glue student photos to them. Place name cards in a gift bag. Choose a name and place it in the blank spot of the sentence strip. Identify the initial sound in the student's name and write it on three index cards to substitute the bolded letters in the song. Then sing "Shake Hands," substituting the student's name and first sound. Move the student's name card down to each line as you sing.

(Use with "Shake Hands," page 16)

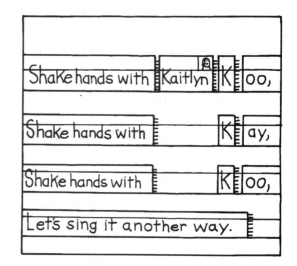

Our School Class Book

Phoneme Substitution

Materials

- "Fun with Names" song (page 17)

- Schoolhouse reproducible (page 80)

- small sticky notes

- bookbinding materials

Write each student's name on the roof of a Schoolhouse reproducible. Give students three small sticky notes, and invite students to write a different letter or letter blend on each sticky note. Have students stack the sticky notes on top of each other and cover the initial letter of their name with the sticky notes to form and then say new words. Invite students to sing "Fun with Names" while flipping up each sticky note, revealing a new letter or letter blend to change their names. Extend the fun by inviting students to decorate their schoolhouse and binding the pages into a class book.

(Use with "Fun with Names," page 17)

Let's Take Roll!
Sound Matching, Phoneme Isolation

In advance, write each student's name on an index card. Each day write on a sentence strip a question such as *Do you have a /b/ in your name?* or *Does your name end with /ee/?* Label two index cards *Yes* and *No* and place them in the top row of a pocket chart. Take roll by showing the class one name card at a

Materials

- index cards
- sentence strips
- pocket chart

time. As students recognize their name, invite them to put their name card in the pocket chart under the appropriate card. Compare the number of children who do and do not have the sound of the day in their name.

(Use with "Name That Sound," page 18)

Does your name start with /j/?	
Yes	**No**
Jacob	Sarah
Jennifer	Emily
Jessica	Mike
Joshua	Ashley
Jonathan	Nicholas
	Brianna
	Austin
	Tyler
	Olivia

Sound Sort
Sound Matching, Phoneme Isolation

Write two or three letters or letter blends on separate index cards and place them in the top row of a pocket chart. Write student names on separate index cards and distribute them to the class. Have students whose names have the same initial sound as one of the letters on the index cards place their name card under that letter. Students whose names do not begin with any of those

Materials

- index cards
- pocket chart

letter sounds place their card in a pile or in a column labeled *No.* Then redistribute cards and have students whose names have the same final sound as one of the letters place their name card under that letter. Finally, have students whose names have the same middle sound as one of the letters place their name card under that letter. The following day, repeat the activity with three new letters.

(Use with "Name That Sound," page 18)

/n/	/k/	/s/
Ian	Brooke	James
Christine	Alec	Thomas
Shannon	Derek	Alexis
Erin	Mark	Charis
Logan		Chris
Ryan		Alice

Silly Names
Phoneme Substitution

Materials

- index cards
- student photos
- glue
- pocket chart

Write student names on index cards and glue student photos to them. Place cards in a pocket chart. Write one capital letter several times on separate index cards. Cover the first letter or letter blend of each student's name with the capital letter. Invite students to read the new silly names. Each day, repeat the activity with a different capital letter.

(Use with "Singing Silly Names," page 19 and "Morning Game," page 21)

Silly-Soup Class Book
Sound Matching

Materials

- Soup Bowl reproducible (page 81)
- crayons or markers
- bookbinding materials

Have students write their name in the first blank of the Soup Bowl reproducible. Then invite students to write or draw three items that have the same initial sound as their name. Bind papers into a class book for rereading.

(Use with "Good Morning," page 20)

In __Lisa__'s silly soup, there are lemons, lizards, and licorice.

Where Can My Good Friend Be?

(sing to the tune of "Where, Oh, Where Has My Little Dog Gone?")

Where, oh, where can my good friend be?

Where, oh, where can she be?

She starts with **/j/** and ends with **/ee/**.

Where, oh, where can she be?

Where, oh, where can my good friend be?

Where, oh, where can he be?

He starts with **/t/** and ends with **/t/**.

Where, oh, where can he be?

Fall Phonemic Awareness Songs & Rhymes © 1998 Creative Teaching Press

Note: Invite students to stand when you give sound clues that match their name. For example, Julie and Judy stand after the first stanza, and Trent stands after the second stanza.

Additional verses: Replace bolded sounds to continue the song.

Friends Sound March

(sing to the tune of "Ants Go Marching")

My friends are marching round and round.

Hurrah, hurrah.

My friends are marching round and round.

Hurrah, hurrah.

My friends are marching round and round

Names beginning with **/b/** must sit on the ground.

We'll march around until we all sit down!

Additional verses: March in a circle and have students whose names begin with the sound you say sit down in the middle of the circle. Continue singing by replacing the bolded sound to continue the song until all students sit down. For example, *Names beginning with /d/ must sit on the ground.*

Fall Phonemic Awareness Songs & Rhymes © 1998 Creative Teaching Press

♫ Buddy Boogie ♫

(sing to the tune of "Hokey Pokey")

Give your pal's hand a shake.

Give your pal's hand a squeeze.

Give your pal a pat,

And then tap him/her on the knees.

You do the Buddy Boogie,

And you turn yourself around.

Friendship's what it's all about.

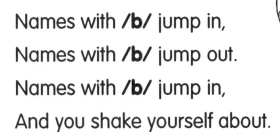

Names with **/b/** jump in,

Names with **/b/** jump out.

Names with **/b/** jump in,

And you shake yourself about.

You do the Buddy Boogie

And you turn yourself around.

/b/ /b/ /b/ /b/ /b/ /b/!

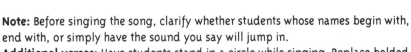

Note: Before singing the song, clarify whether students whose names begin with, end with, or simply have the sound you say will jump in.

Additional verses: Have students stand in a circle while singing. Replace bolded sounds to continue the song. For example, *Names with /m/ jump in.* Repeat second stanza until all students have had a turn.

Who's My Friend?

(sing to the tune of "Three Blind Mice")

Who's my friend?

Who's my friend?

Can you pick the one?

Can you pick the one?

My friend has a name that starts with /l/.

Do you know which friend it could be?

Carol, Walter, or **Luca?**

Carol, Walter, or **Luca?**

Who's my friend?

Who's my friend?

Can you pick the one?

Can you pick the one?

My friend has a name that ends with /n/.

Do you know which friend it could be?

Nancy, Austin, or **Tania?**

Nancy, Austin, or **Tania?**

Additional verses: Replace bolded names and sounds to continue the song. Use student names from your class.

Fall Phonemic Awareness Songs & Rhymes © 1998 Creative Teaching Press

Where Is My Friend?

(sing to the tune of "Are You Sleeping?")

Where is **/M/ /a/ /t/**?
Where is **/M/ /a/ /t/**?
Here I am.
Here I am.

How is our good friend today?
How is our good friend today?
I am fine.
I am fine.

Note: Have the appropriate student respond to the questions.
Additional verses: Replace bolded name to continue the song. For example,
sing *Where is /J/ /e/ /f/?* and have Jeff respond.

I Have a New Friend

(sing to the tune of "Skip to My Lou")

I have a new friend. Yes, I do.
I have a new friend. Yes, I do.
I have a new friend. Yes, I do.
Can you guess his/her name?

My friend's name starts with **/m/**.
My friend's name starts with **/m/**.
My friend's name starts with **/m/**.
Can you guess his/her name?

My friend's name rhymes with **hat**.
My friend's name rhymes with **hat**.
My friend's name rhymes with **hat**.
Can you guess his/her name?

Additional verses: Replace bolded sounds and words to continue the song. For example, *My friend's name rhymes with **bike**.*

Fall Phonemic Awareness Songs & Rhymes © 1998 Creative Teaching Press

Share with You

(sing to the tune of "A-Tisket, A-Tasket")

I'll share with you.

You share with me.

And we can be friends, you'll agree.

When I share my **snack** with **Sarah,**

A better friend I will be.

Additional verses: Replace the bolded words with an item and a name that
begin with the same sound. For example, *When I share my* **crayons** *with* **Chris,**
a better friend I will be.

Guess My Friend

Syllable Counting, Phoneme Isolation

Materials

- index cards

- student photos

- glue

- hat

Write each student's name on an index card, glue his or her photo on it, and place the cards in a hat. Secretly select a card from the hat. Clap the number of syllables in the child's name and ask students to guess whose name it could be. If necessary, help the class narrow it down by telling them the beginning and/or ending sound in the name. For example, you could choose *Melody* and clap three times. Students could guess *Erika, Kimberly,* and *Jonathan.* Then you may say *My friend's name begins with /m/.* They could guess *Monica.* Then you

could say *My friend's name ends with /ee/.* Once the class guesses *Melody,* show the photo name card and have students clap the three syllables in her name together. Continue with other names.

(Use with "Where Can My Good Friend Be?" page 25)

Mirror, Mirror, on the Wall

Sound Matching

Materials

- aluminum foil

- paper plates

- construction paper

- glue

- art supplies (glitter, colored macaroni, confetti, paint, paintbrushes)

- tongue depressors

Have each student cover the center of a paper plate with aluminum foil to make a "mirror." Ask students to paint a self-portrait on construction paper and glue it to the foil background. Invite students to decorate the border with various craft items such as glitter and colored macaroni. Have students glue a tongue-depressor "handle" to the back of the paper-plate mirror. Ask students to write their name below their picture and write on the back side of the mirror (or dictate as you write) why they are a good friend. Then, invite the student of the day to choose a sound and have him or her say *Mirror, mirror, on the wall . . . show me names that start with* (selected sound)—*show them all.* Ask students whose names begin with the chosen sound to hold up their mirror. Continue the game until all students have a turn. Extend the fun by displaying mirrors on a bulletin-board display titled *Mirror, Mirror, on the Wall . . . We Are Friendly One and All.*

(Use with "Friends Sound March," page 26)

Find a Friend
Sound Matching

Distribute copies of the Boy/Girl reproducible to the class. Have students decorate the boy/girl, cut it out, and print their name on the front of the doll. Invite students to find classmates who share the same initial sound in their name. If they are unable to find a classmate, invite students to find a classroom object or puppet that shares the same initial sound. Use the paper dolls throughout the year for other activities, such as graphing and sorting.

(Use with "Buddy Boogie," page 27)

(Use with "Buddy Boogie," page 27)

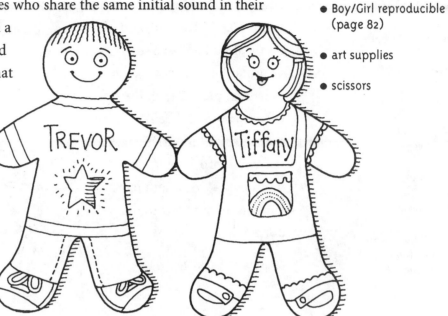

Materials

- Boy/Girl reproducible (page 82)
- art supplies
- scissors

Telephone Talk
Sound Matching

Ask students to sit in a circle. Give one student a telephone and have him or her say one word into it. The phone is then passed to the child on his or her right who says another word beginning with the same sound. For example, if the first student says *turtle*, the next student could say *table*. Challenge the class to "pass the sound" around the circle without saying the same word twice.

(Use with "Buddy Boogie," page 27)

(Use with "Buddy Boogie," page 27)

Spaghetti...

Materials

- play telephone

The Picnic

Sound Matching

Materials

- index cards
- student photos
- glue
- picnic basket
- magazines or newspapers
- scissors
- tablecloth
- plastic utensils, play food, napkins (optional)

Write each student's name on an index card, glue his or her photo on it, and place the cards in a picnic basket. Have students cut out from magazines or newspapers food pictures that begin with the same sound as their name, glue them to an index card, and place them in the picnic basket. Place a tablecloth on the floor and have students sit around it. Invite students to have a "picnic" with their friends and serve their friends the matching "foods." For even more fun, provide plastic utensils, play food, and paper napkins for students to use during their "meal."

(Use with "Who's My Friend?" page 28)

Food and Friends Memory Match

Sound Matching

Materials

- food and name cards from The Picnic activity (above)

Mix the food and name cards used in The Picnic activity and spread them out facedown on the floor. Invite students to take turns flipping over a name card and a food card. If they both begin with the same sound, the student keeps them. If not, the student returns the cards facedown and another student gets a turn. The game ends when all matches are found.

(Use with "Who's My Friend?" page 28)

Our Friends

Syllable Splitting, Phoneme Blending, Phoneme Segmentation

Write each student's name on an index card, glue his or her photo on it, and place the cards in a hat or basket. Choose a card and separate each sound in the student's name or divide the name into onset and rime. For example, /B/ /r/ /a/ /d/ or /K/—ayla. Have students blend the sounds together to name the student. Show students the photo name card after students say the correct name. This is a great activity for dismissing students to lunch or recess. For a greater challenge, invite students to segment their class-mates' names and hold up the photo name card after the class says the correct name.

(Use with "Where Is My Friend?" page 29)

(Use with "Where Is My Friend?" page 29)

Materials

- index cards
- student photos
- glue
- hat or basket

Count the Sounds

Phoneme Counting, Phoneme Segmentation

Glue student photos onto separate index cards. Hold up one photo card. Have students sing "Where Is My Friend?" and separate the sounds in that child's

name. For example, *Where is* /Ch/ /a/ /d/? Ask students to count with their fingers in the air as they say each sound. For example, Chad has three sounds and Brad has four sounds. Then have that student answer. Continue singing the song with other students' names.

(Use with "Where Is My Friend?" page 29)

(Use with "Where Is My Friend?" page 29)

Materials

- "Where Is My Friend?" song (page 29)
- student photos
- index cards
- glue

Roll a Rhyme

Rhyming, Sound Matching

Materials

● ball

Have students sit in a circle. Give one student a ball and ask him or her to say a word that starts with the same sound as his or her name and then roll the ball to a friend. The student who receives the ball says a word that rhymes with that word. (Remind students that rhyming words can be nonsense words.) Then, that student says a new word that starts with the same sound as his or her name and rolls the ball to a new friend. Continue playing until all students have a turn.

(Use with "I Have a New Friend," page 30)

We-Can-Share Paper Dolls

Sound Matching, Phoneme Isolation

Materials

● butcher paper

● scissors

● crayons or markers

Cut from butcher paper a giant paper doll for each student to decorate. Brainstorm different items children can share that begin with the same sound as their name and write it on each student's paper doll. For example, *Trenton shares trucks, Kay shares cookies, Brenden shares books.* Read the text aloud with the class. For extra fun, post the paper dolls as part of a motivational bulletin-board display.

(Use with "Share with You," page 31)

It's September

(sing to the tune of "Twinkle, Twinkle, Little Star")

It's September, fall is here.

It's my favorite time of year.

Boys and girls make new friends.

Teachers lend a helping hand.

Lots to learn and so much fun.

Back to school for everyone.

♫ Picking Up Pumpkins

(sing to the tune of "Ten Little Indians")

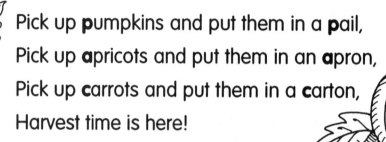

Pick up **p**umpkins and put them in a **p**ail,

Pick up **a**pricots and put them in an **a**pron,

Pick up **c**arrots and put them in a **c**arton,

Harvest time is here!

Pick up **s**eeds and put them in a **s**ack,

Pick up **b**eets and put them in a **b**ag,

Pick up **p**ecans and put them in a **p**ie,

Harvest time is here!

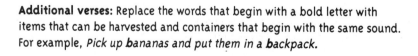

Additional verses: Replace the words that begin with a bold letter with items that can be harvested and containers that begin with the same sound. For example, *Pick up bananas and put them in a backpack.*

I See Apples

(sing to the tune of "Clementine")

I see apples.

I see apples.

I see apples on a tree.

We can count them all together.

Some for you,

And some for me.

Some are **r–ed.**

Some are **/y/ /e/ /l/ /ow/.**

Some are **/g/ /r/ /ee/ /n/,** too.

We can count them all together.

Some for me,

And some for you.

Some rhyme with **bean.**

Some rhyme with **cello.**

Some rhyme with **bed,** too.

We can count them all together.

Some for me,

And some for you.

Additional verses: Replace the bolded phonemes with other color words. For example, *Some are **br–own.***
Replace the bolded words with words that rhyme with the new color words. For example, *Some rhyme with **down.***

Fall Phonemic Awareness Songs & Rhymes © 1998 Creative Teaching Press

Favorite Colors

(sing to the tune of "Six Little Ducks")

So many crayons in the box for you,

Red ones, yellow ones, blue ones, too.

But the one little crayon that rhymes with **bean**

Is my favorite color.

It's the color **green.**

Additional verses: Replace the first bolded word with a new word that rhymes
with a color word. For example, *But the one little crayon that rhymes with **shoe**
is my favorite color. It's the color **blue.***

My Lunch Box
(sing to the tune of "Yankee Doodle")

My lunch box holds some yummy treats.

Which food is my favorite?

It starts with **sand** and ends with **wich.**

A sandwich! Now I'll eat it.

My lunch box holds some yummy treats.

Which drink is my favorite?

It starts with **/m/** and ends with **ilk.**

My milk! Now I'll drink it.

My lunch box holds some yummy treats.

Which food is my favorite?

It starts with **/ch/** and ends with **ips.**

Some chips! Now I'll eat them.

My lunch box holds some yummy treats.

Which food is my favorite?

It starts with **cook** and ends with **ies.**

Some cookies! Now I'll eat them.

Additional verses: Replace the bolded sounds and words with new food items.
For example, *It starts with **/ch/** and ends with **eese. Some cheese!** Now I'll eat it.*

♫ Apples ♫

(sing to the tune of "On Top of Old Smokey")

I love to eat apples.

They're juicy and sweet.

The one thing I don't know,

Is which one to eat.

Red, yellow, and green,

They're all good for me.

If you had to choose one,

Which one would it be?

I love to eat **b**apples.

They're **b**uicy and **b**weet.

The one thing I don't know,

Is which one to eat.

Bed, **b**ellow, and **b**reen,

They're all good for me.

If you had to choose one,

Which one would it be?

Additional verses: Replace the bolded letter with a new letter to continue the song. For example, *I love to eat tapples. They're tuicy and tweet.*

Fall Phonemic Awareness Songs & Rhymes © 1998 Creative Teaching Press

September Spinning Game
Sound Matching

Copy the Spinner reproducible and the Back-to-School Picture Cards on card stock. Use a brad to attach a paper-clip "pointer" to the center of the spinner. Lay the picture cards faceup on the floor or a table. Invite students to take

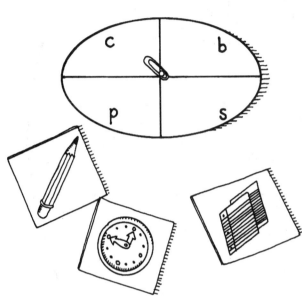

turns spinning the spinner. Have them identify the letter the spinner lands on, say the letter sound, and find a picture card that begins with that sound. If none of the remaining cards match the sound, then the next player takes his or her turn. The game is over when all picture cards are collected.

(Use with "It's September," page 37)

(Use with "It's September," page 37)

Materials

- Spinner reproducible (page 83)
- Back-to-School Picture Cards (page 84)
- card stock
- gold brad
- paper clip

Garden Time
Sound Matching

Sing "Picking Up Pumpkins" with your students. Then ask the class what they would pick from a garden. Distribute copies of the Wheelbarrow reproducible, and have students draw a picture of an item from the garden and an item to put it in that begins with the same sound. Or, invite students to cut out pictures of items that begin with the same sound and glue them on the reproducible. For example, *Pick up **beans** and put them in a **basket**.* Invite students to share their papers with the class. Bind pages into a class garden book.

(Use with "Picking Up Pumpkins," page 38)

(Use with "Picking Up Pumpkins," page 38)

Pick up bananas and put them in a barrel.

Materials

- "Picking Up Pumpkins" song (page 38)
- Wheelbarrow reproducible (page 85)
- crayons or markers
- glue
- bookbinding materials

Worm and Apple Game
Sound Matching

Materials

- Worm Picture Cards (page 86)
- Apple Picture Cards (page 87)
- colored paper (2 colors)
- picnic blanket

Have students sit in a circle. Photocopy the Worm and Apple Picture Cards on different colored paper. Lay the cards picture-side down on a picnic blanket. Have students take turns flipping over an apple and a worm card to find picture pairs that end with the same sound. The game is over when all matches are found.

(Use with "I See Apples," page 39)

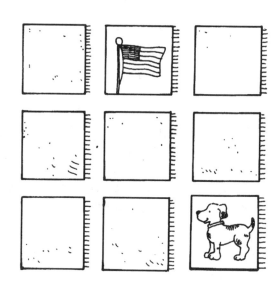

Color Rhymes
Rhyming

Materials

- "Favorite Colors" song (page 40)
- construction paper
- scissors
- crayons

Cut out large "crayons" from various colors of construction paper and distribute them to students. Sing "Favorite Colors" with your students. At the end of the song, have the student with the construction-paper crayon that rhymes with the rhyming word in the song hold it up. To involve all students, have students set their own crayons on their desk and hold up the crayon whose color rhymes with the rhyming word.

(Use with "Favorite Colors," page 40)

Lunch-Box Sorting

Sound Matching, Phoneme Isolation

Invite partners to sort food in their lunches by beginning sounds. For example, *bologna* and *banana* would be grouped together. Have students brainstorm a list of other foods that belong in each food group. For a greater challenge, have partners sort food items by ending sounds, such as *sandwich* and *peach.*

(Use with "My Lunch Box," page 41)

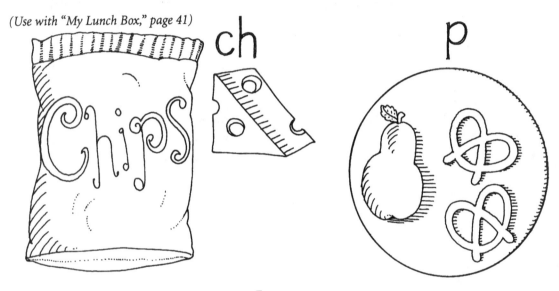

Apples in a Basket

Phoneme Substitution

Write a consonant on separate apple cutouts and place them in a basket. Invite a volunteer to pull an apple from the basket. Then, sing "Apples" with the class, substituting the new letter sound. Pass the basket for another student to choose an apple with a new sound to substitute.

(Use with "Apples," page 42)

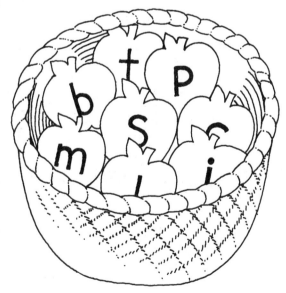

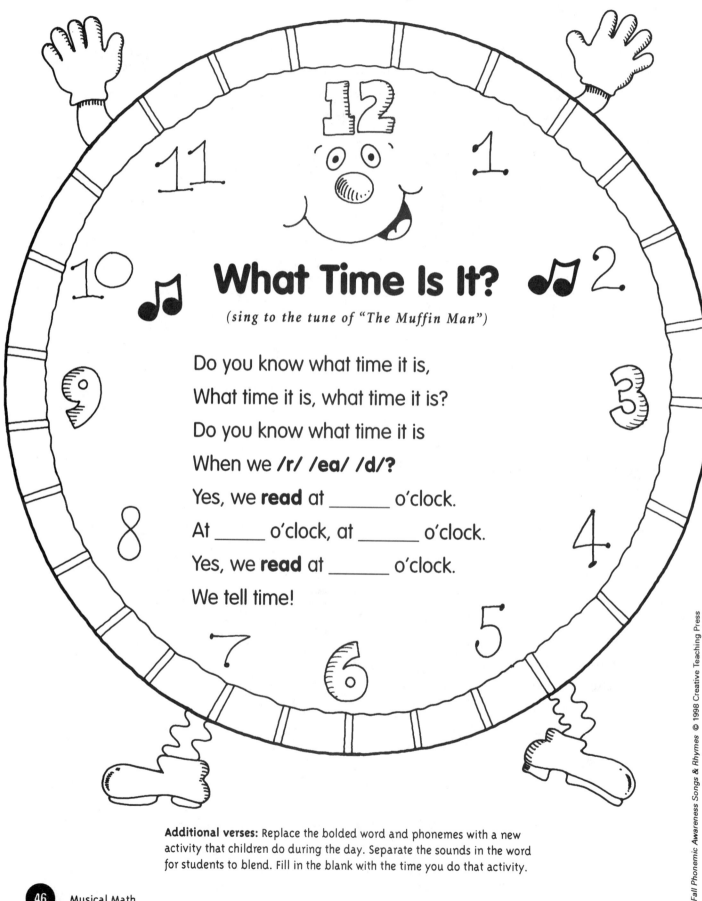

What Time Is It?

(sing to the tune of "The Muffin Man")

Do you know what time it is,

What time it is, what time it is?

Do you know what time it is

When we **/r/ /ea/ /d/?**

Yes, we **read** at _____ o'clock.

At _____ o'clock, at _____ o'clock.

Yes, we **read** at _____ o'clock.

We tell time!

Additional verses: Replace the bolded word and phonemes with a new activity that children do during the day. Separate the sounds in the word for students to blend. Fill in the blank with the time you do that activity.

Fall Phonemic Awareness Songs & Rhymes © 1998 Creative Teaching Press

A-Counting We Will Go

(sing to the tune of "A-Hunting We Will Go")

A-counting we will go,

A-counting we will go,

We'll count each item one by one

And put them in a row.

Let's count to number **/f/ /i/ /v/.**

Let's count to number **five.**

Let's count the **foxes** up to **five**

And put them in a row.

Additional verses: Replace the bolded words and phonemes with a different number and an item that begins with the same sound as the number. Separate each sound in the number. For example, *Let's count to number /n/ /i/ /n/. Let's count to number **nine.** Let's count the **nuts** up to **nine** and put them in a row.*

Clapping Patterns

(sing to the tune of "Are You Sleeping?")

Clap a friend's name.
Clap a friend's name.
After me.
After me.
Clapping names is so much fun
Especially clapping this new one:

Sa-man-tha
Sa-man-tha.

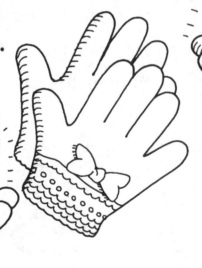

Note: Chant and clap the syllables in each student's name for children to repeat.
Additional verses: Replace bolded words with other actions such as snapping, marching, tapping, or whistling to sing additional verses. For example, ***Snap*** a friend's name or ***Tap*** a friend's name. Then snap your fingers or tap your toes as you say the child's name in syllables.

Fall Phonemic Awareness Songs & Rhymes © 1998 Creative Teaching Press

I Like to Sort

(sing to the tune of "Apples and Bananas")

I like to sort, sort, sort,

By letter sounds.

I like to sort, sort, sort,

By letter sounds.

Let's sort the **p**lay dough, **b**ooks, and **s**cissors.

Let's sort the **p**encils, **b**locks, and **s**tickers.

Let's sort the **p**uppets, **b**ears, and **s**tring.

We can sort so many classroom things.

♫ Can You Make a Number Rhyme? ♫

(sing to the tune of "Oscar Mayer Wiener")

Oh, who would like to make a number rhyme?
I think it would be really, really fun!
If you'd like to make a number rhyme,
Can you make a rhyme for number one?

Oh, who would like to make a number rhyme?
I think it would be really fun to do!
If you'd like to make a number rhyme,
Can you make a rhyme for number two?

Oh, who would like to make a number rhyme?
I think it is as easy as can be!
If you'd like to make a number rhyme,
Can you make a rhyme for number three?

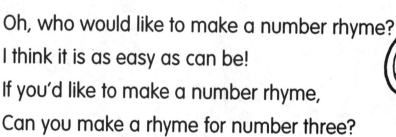

Oh, who would like to make a number rhyme?
I wonder who can think of any more!
If you'd like to make a number rhyme,
Can you make a rhyme for number four?

Note: Invite students to call out rhyming words after each stanza.

Fall Phonemic Awareness Songs & Rhymes © 1998 Creative Teaching Press

My Clock
Phoneme Blending, Phoneme Segmentation

Have students cut out the Tick-Tock Clock reproducible and glue it to the front of a paper plate. Help students put a brad and the clock hands in the center of the plate. As they sing "What Time Is It?" have students manipulate the clock hands to show the times they do certain activities. Invite volunteers to separate the sounds in the name of an activity as they sing the song. For example, *Do you know what time it is when we /ea/ /t/ /l/ /u/ /n/ /ch/?*

(Use with "What Time Is It?" page 46)

Materials

- "What Time Is It?" song (page 46)
- Tick-Tock Clock reproducible (page 88)
- paper plates
- scissors
- glue
- gold brads

We Can Count
Phoneme Substitution

Copy on sentence strips the words to "A-Counting We Will Go" and place them in a pocket chart. Photocopy the Counting Picture Cards and invite students to place the cards in the pocket chart as the class sings "A-Counting We Will Go." Then, invite students to substitute the onset (all the sounds in a word that come before the first vowel) of the item they are counting with a different letter or letter blend. For example, students can change *Let's count the fishes up to four* to *Let's count the dishes up to four.* Invite students to make nonsense words, too; for example, *Let's count the mishes up to four.*

(Use with "A-Counting We Will Go," page 47)

Materials

- "A-Counting We Will Go" song (page 47)
- Counting Picture Cards (page 89)
- sentence strips
- pocket chart

Living Patterns
Syllable Counting

Materials

● none

To form a "living pattern," select students whose names fit a pattern to stand in a row in front of the class. For example, have a student with a two-syllable name stand next to a student with a three-syllable name, then a student with a two-syllable name, etc. Have the class clap out the names and guess the "mystery pattern."

(Use with "Clapping Patterns," page 48)

Keep the Rhythm Game
Syllable Counting

Materials

● none

Ask students to sit cross-legged in a circle on the floor. Have students tap their laps twice and then clap their hands, tap their laps twice and then clap their hands. Continue the pattern until all students have the rhythm. To begin the game, say your name (divided into syllables) as you clap your hands. Then tap your lap twice and say a student's name (divided into syllables) as you clap your hands. That student then continues the pattern and says his or her own name (divided into syllables) while clapping his or her hands, and then says another student's name. Continue playing until all students have had a chance to lead.

(Use with "Clapping Patterns," page 48)

Classroom Sorting

Sound Matching

Write on three separate index cards a different letter. Place three hula hoops or large circles of yarn on the floor. Place inside each hoop an index card with a different letter. Invite students to find objects in the classroom that begin with the same sound as the letter in each hoop and then place the objects in the correct hoop.

(Use with "I Like to Sort," page 49)

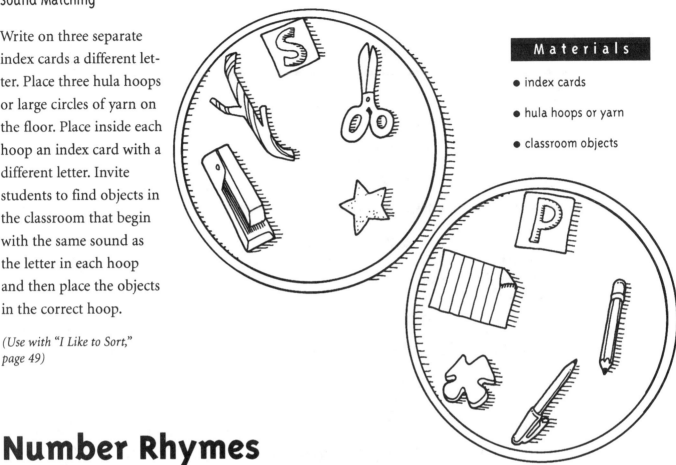

Materials

- index cards
- hula hoops or yarn
- classroom objects

Number Rhymes

Rhyming

Glue each numeral to the top corner of a separate sheet of construction paper. Divide the class into ten small groups. Give each group a construction-paper sheet and have the group illustrate a number rhyme that matches the number on its sheet. For example, ***Three*** *bees in a* ***tree*** or ***Four*** *spiders on a* ***door.*** Bind these pages together to create a number rhyming book or hang them on a wire across your room for students to reread.

(Use with "Can You Make a Number Rhyme?" page 50)

Materials

- die-cut numerals (1–10)
- glue
- construction paper
- crayons or markers
- bookbinding materials or wire

It's Halloween Night

(sing to the tune of "The Farmer in the Dell")

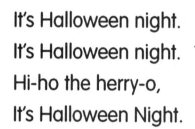

It's Halloween night.
It's Halloween night.
Hi-ho the herry-o,
It's Halloween Night.

I think I see a bat.
I think I see a bat.
Bi-bo the berry-o,
I think I see a bat.

Now I see a scarecrow.
Now I see a scarecrow.
Si-so the serry-o,
Now I see a scarecrow.

Oh, is that a monster?
Oh, is that a monster?
Mi-mo the merry-o,
Oh, is that a monster?

I think it's time to go.
I think it's time to go.
Gi-go the gerry-o,
I think it's time to go.
Good-bye!

Fall Phonemic Awareness Songs & Rhymes © 1998 Creative Teaching Press

Five Little Pumpkins

(sing to the tune of "Six Little Ducks")

Five little pumpkins

That I once knew,

Fat ones, tall ones, scary ones, too.

But the one little pumpkin

With the candle shining bright,

He scared the **/c/ /a/ /t/**

On Halloween night!

Additional verses: Replace the bolded phonemes with other items the pumpkins could scare. For example, *He scared the /m/ /u/ /m/ /ee/ on Halloween night!*

♫ Bats ♫

(sing to the tune of "The Beverly Hillbillies")

One, one, one, bats have lots of fun.

Two, two, two, bats can shout, "Boo!"

Three, three, three, bats hang in a tree.

Four, four, four, bats can soar.

Five, five, five, bats can really dive.

Six, six, six, bats can carry sticks.

Seven, seven, seven, bats fly straight to heaven.

Eight, eight, eight, bats sit on a gate.

Nine, nine, nine, bats are feeling fine.

Ten, ten, ten, let's count them all again.

Ten, nine, eight, seven, six, five, four,

Three, two, one—the bats had fun!

Fall Phonemic Awareness Songs & Rhymes © 1998 Creative Teaching Press

My Spooky House

(sing to the tune of "The Farmer in the Dell")

This spooky house is mine.

This spooky house is mine.

Have you ever seen a house as spooky as mine?

My house has a **/b/ /a/ /t/.**

Yes, my house has a **bat.**

Have you ever seen a house as spooky as mine?

Additional verses: Replace the bolded word and phonemes with other "spooky" items.
Separate the letter sounds for students to blend. For example, *My house has a /gh/ /o/ /s/ /t/.*

What I Spy in the Night

(sing to the tune of "Itsy Bitsy Spider")

Here is a song about some creatures in the night.

And different things that might give you a fright.

I'll say words that are missing the first sound.

When you say the secret words, the creatures will be found.

If I spy an **onster,** you know it's a _____.

Now I spy an **at.** You know it's a _____.

Next, I spy an **arecrow.** You know it's a _____.

Finally, I spy a **host.** Yes, it is a _____.

Boo!

Note: Have students add the missing phoneme and say the complete word to fill in the blank.

Fall Phonemic Awareness Songs & Rhymes © 1998 Creative Teaching Press

Halloween Songbook
Phoneme Substitution

Place a photocopy of the Halloween Picture Cards in a pumpkin bucket. Invite student groups to choose a card from the bucket. Have each group use their card to create a new verse for "It's Halloween Night." Copy the verses onto construction paper, and have students decorate each page. Bind the pages into a class songbook.

(Use with "It's Halloween Night," page 54)

Materials

- "It's Halloween Night" song (page 54)
- Halloween Picture Cards (page 90)
- pumpkin bucket
- construction paper
- bookbinding materials

I think I see a spider.
I think I see a spider.
Si-so the serry-o,
I think I see a spider.

Halloween Ball Class Book
Sound Matching

Take photographs of each student in his or her Halloween costume. Invite students to sort the photographs by the name, color, style, beginning sound, or ending sound of the costume, or by whether or not the costume is scary. Glue each photo to construction paper and write the sentence frame _____ *came as a _____ to the Halloween Ball.* Have students write their name and a word to describe themselves that begins with the same sound as their name in the first blank. Have them write the name of their costume in the second blank. For example, ***Silly Steve** came as a **bumblebee** to the Halloween Ball.* Bind the pages into a class book and title it *Halloween Ball.*

(Use with "It's Halloween Night," page 54)

Materials

- camera and film
- glue
- construction paper
- bookbinding materials

Silly Steve came as a bumblebee to the Halloween Ball.

Pumpkin Patch

Phoneme Blending, Phoneme Segmentation

Materials

- "Five Little Pumpkins" song (page 55)
- Halloween Picture Cards (page 90)
- scissors

Photocopy the Halloween Picture Cards, cut them apart, and distribute them to a few volunteers. Invite the volunteers to hold their card behind their back. Then sing "Five Little Pumpkins" with your class. When you get to the part of the song with the bolded phonemes, invite one volunteer to separate the sounds of the name of the item on his or her card and have the rest of the class blend the word.

(Use with "Five Little Pumpkins," page 55)

Spin a Web

Sound Matching, Phoneme Deletion

Materials

- ball of string

Have students sit in a circle. Toss a ball of string to a child. Ask that student to say a word that begins with the same sound as *spider* (/s/). That child then tosses the string to another student while holding on to one end. The new student says another word beginning with /s/. The game continues until all students have spun the web. Challenge the class to say a new /s/ word that has not already been said. Play the game again using a different beginning sound. For phoneme deletion practice, have each student say a word with the first sound deleted, such as *pider,* before tossing the ball of string. The child who catches the string adds a beginning sound to make a word (*spider*). The child then says a new word with a deleted first sound, such as *umpkin,* before tossing the string. The child who catches it would say *pumpkin.*

(Use with "Five Little Pumpkins," page 55)

Bats in the Belfry
Sound Matching, Phoneme Substitution

Bats in the belfry.

Invite students to trace the Bat reproducible onto black construction paper. Have each student glue a bat to a 3" x 18" (7.5 cm x 46 cm) black construction-paper strip to form a bat hat. Help students hole-punch each end of the strip, put in gold brads, and hook a rubber band around the fasteners. Have students wear their hats while singing "Bats." Then have all students form a circle. Invite one child to "fly" to the center and call out *Bats in the belfry*. Then that child chooses another child to "fly" to the center. This child changes *bats* to his or her first name and chooses a place that begins with the same sound. For example, *Cara's in the kitchen* or *Mike's at the mall*. That student then chooses another student to "fly" to the center and call out a new phrase. Continue playing until all bats get to fly!

(Use with "Bats," page 56)

Materials
- "Bats" song (page 56)
- Bat reproducible (page 91)
- black construction paper
- glue
- hole punch
- gold brads
- rubber bands

Flying Bats
Phoneme Blending

Invite each student to color and cut out a photocopy of the Bat reproducible. Have students fold the bat in half, hole-punch near the fold, and thread $1/3$ of a pipe cleaner through the hole to form a ring. Give half of the class an onset (a consonant or blend) and give the rest of the students a rime (the ending of a word). For example, one student will have the onset *b* and another student will have the rime *at*. Together, they make *bat*. Play Halloween background music while the bats "fly" around whispering out their "bat call" (their onset or rime). Each student must find a bat partner to make a complete word. After everyone finds a partner, invite pairs to blend their new word for everyone to hear.

(Use with "Bats," page 56)

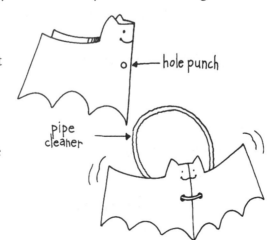

hole punch

pipe cleaner

Materials
- Bat reproducible (page 91)
- crayons or markers
- scissors
- hole punch
- pipe cleaners
- Halloween background music

Spooky House
Phoneme Blending, Phoneme Segmentation

Materials

- "My Spooky House" song (page 57)
- Halloween Picture Cards (page 90)
- scissors
- paper lunch sacks
- crayons or markers

Cut the top corners of paper lunch sacks so the center comes to a point, and give a sack to each student. Invite students to decorate their paper sack like a "spooky house." Give each student a photocopy of the Halloween Picture

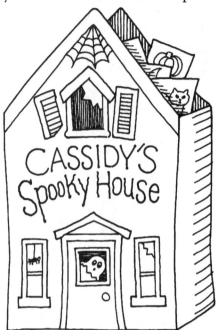

Cards. Have students cut the cards apart and place them inside their spooky house. As students sing "My Spooky House," invite a volunteer to pull out a card, and have the class orally separate the sounds in the picture's name and then blend the word.

(Use with "My Spooky House," page 57)

I Spy
Phoneme Deletion

Materials

- "What I Spy in the Night" song (page 58)
- Halloween Picture Cards (page 90)
- index cards
- pocket chart

Write on index cards the words *onster, at, arecrow,* and *host* and place the cards in a pocket chart. Write on separate index cards the letters *m, b, sc,* and *g*. As students sing "What I Spy in the Night," invite volunteers to select the correct beginning sounds (the onsets) that match the correct ending sounds (the rimes) in the pocket chart. Ask students to hold up the correct Halloween Picture Card that matches the word and have a volunteer place it in the pocket chart next to the matching word. Have students take turns adding the missing onset and showing the matching picture.

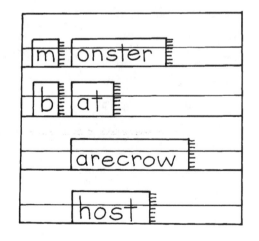

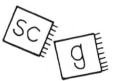

(Use with "What I Spy in the Night," page 58)

What's Cooking in the Kitchen?

(sing to the tune of "For He's a Jolly Good Fellow")

What's cooking in the kitchen?
What's cooking in the kitchen?
What's cooking in the kitchen
That rhymes with **head?** (bread)

What's cooking in the kitchen?
What's cooking in the kitchen?
What's cooking in the kitchen
That rhymes with **horn?** (corn)

What's cooking in the kitchen?
What's cooking in the kitchen?
What's cooking in the kitchen
That rhymes with **perky?** (turkey)

Additional verses: Replace the bolded words with words that rhyme with a Thanksgiving food. For example, *What's cooking in the kitchen that rhymes with **rye?** (pie)*

Fall Phonemic Awareness Songs & Rhymes © 1998 Creative Teaching Press

Mr. Turkey

(sing to the tune of "Clementine")

Mr. **T**urkey, Mr. **T**urkey,
Are you ready to eat?
If you came to Thanksgiving dinner,
What kind of food would be your treat?

Would you like **tacos,**
Tapioca, tuna, or **tea?**
Tell me all of your favorites
You would like to eat with me.

Additional verses: Replace the beginning sound of /t/ in *Mr. Turkey* with another sound. For example, *Mr. Surkey* or *Mr. Churkey.* Then, substitute the bolded words with foods that start with that same beginning sound.

Fall Phonemic Awareness Songs & Rhymes © 1998 Creative Teaching Press

Turkey Talk

(sing to the tune of "The Wheels on the Bus")

Tell me the first sound that you hear,

That you hear,

That you hear.

Tell me the first sound that you hear in

Turkey, turkey, turkey.

Tell me the last sound that you hear,

That you hear,

That you hear.

Tell me the last sound that you hear in

Turkey, turkey, turkey.

Tell me the middle sound that you hear,

That you hear,

That you hear.

Tell me the middle sound that you hear in

Turkey, turkey, turkey.

Note: Students respond after each stanza.

Additional verses: Replace the bolded word with other Thanksgiving-related words to continue the song. For example, *Tell me the first sound that you hear in* **pilgrim, pilgrim, pilgrim.**

Tommy the Turkey

(sing to the tune of "On Top of Old Smokey")

Meet Tommy the Turkey.
He starts words with Ts.

When he asks for **tapples,**
Give him **apples,** please.

When he asks for **talad,**
Give him **salad,** please.

When he asks for **totatoes,**
Give him **potatoes,** please.

Additional verses: Replace the bolded words with other foods. Substitute the initial sound of the new words with /t/, and have students say the name of the food. For a greater challenge, invite a student volunteer to substitute the initial sound of a food with /t/ and have the class say the name of the food.

Fall Phonemic Awareness Songs & Rhymes © 1998 Creative Teaching Press

Thanksgiving Dinner

(sing to the tune of "Three Blind Mice")

Thanksgiving dinner.
Thanksgiving dinner.
What will we eat?
What will we eat?

Suzy will eat **salad** and **soup**,
Peter will eat **potatoes** and **peas**,
Tim will eat **turkey** and **tarts**,
For Thanksgiving dinner.

Additional verses: Replace the bolded names and words with children's names from your class and foods that begin with the same sound. For example, *Bill will eat **bananas** and **bread***.

Fall Phonemic Awareness Songs & Rhymes © 1998 Creative Teaching Press

Let's Give Thanks

(sing to the tune of "The Wheels on the Bus")

Let's give thanks for all we have,

All we have, all we have.

Let's give thanks for all we have.

Katie is thankful for **kittens.**

Additional verses: Replace the bolded name and word with student names and items they are thankful for that begin with the same sound as their name. For example, *Denise is thankful for daisies.*

Fall Phonemic Awareness Songs & Rhymes © 1998 Creative Teaching Press

What's Cooking?
Rhyming

Put real or plastic food items in a pasta or soup pot and create a rhyming word for each item. As you sing "What's Cooking in the Kitchen?" with the class, pause for the children to guess the food item that rhymes with the last word you sing. For example, *What's cooking in the kitchen that rhymes with red? (pause) bread.* Then, pull that food item out of the pot for the class to see.

(Use with "What's Cooking in the Kitchen?" page 63)

Materials

● "What's Cooking in the Kitchen?" song (page 63)

● pasta or soup pot

● real or plastic food items

Mr. Turkey Eats
Sound Matching, Phoneme Substitution

Have students color and cut out the Mr. Turkey reproducible. Have students glue their turkey to a paper lunch sack and cut a hole in the sack behind the turkey's mouth. Invite them to substitute the initial sound in *turkey* to give their turkey a name. Have students cut out from magazines pictures of foods that begin with the same initial sound as their turkey and glue them on index cards. Invite students to put the foods into their turkey's mouth as they say the food names. For example, *Churkey the Turkey eats cheese, chicken, and chili.*

(Use with "Mr. Turkey," page 64)

Materials

● Mr. Turkey reproducible (page 92)

● crayons or markers

● scissors

● glue

● paper lunch sacks

● magazines

● index cards

T . . . T . . . Turkey

Sound Matching, Phoneme Isolation

Materials

● "Turkey Talk" song (page 65)

● individual chalkboards or paper

As you sing "Turkey Talk" with your class, have each student write on an individual chalkboard or sheet of paper the first, middle, or last sound in the bolded word in the song. After giving the class "think time," ask them to show you their board or paper. Continue singing the song using other words.

(Use with "Turkey Talk," page 65)

Treats for Turkey

Sound Matching, Phoneme Addition, Phoneme Substitution

Materials

● "Tommy the Turkey" song (page 66)

Have students sing "Tommy the Turkey." After students are familiar with the song, choose a student volunteer to replace *Tommy* with his or her name and replace *Turkey* with an animal that begins with the same sound as his or her name. For example, *Meet Barbara the Badger. She starts words with Bs.* Invite the class to sing the song with the new name and to add or substitute the new sound for the foods. For example, *When she asks for bapples, give her apples, please.* Continue singing with other students' names.

(Use with "Tommy the Turkey," page 66)

♫ Meet Carly the Camel. She starts words with Cs. ♫

Our Thanksgiving Menu
Sound Matching

Have students draw on construction paper a self-portrait and food items that begin with the same sound as their name. Write below each picture *(Student's name) will eat (name of foods)*. For example, *Jonah will eat jam and jelly beans*. Bind pages into a class book for students to reread.

(Use with "Thanksgiving Dinner," page 67)

Materials

- construction paper
- crayons or markers
- bookbinding materials

We're Thankful Class Book
Sound Matching

Glue a photo of each student on separate sheets of construction paper. Ask students to draw something next to their photo that they are thankful for that begins with the same sound as their name. For example, *Zoe is thankful for zebras*. Bind the papers into a class book titled *We're Thankful*.

(Use with "Let's Give Thanks," page 68)

Materials

- student photos
- glue
- construction paper
- crayons or markers
- bookbinding materials

I Saw an Owl

(sing to the tune of "Clementine")

I saw an owl,

A baby owl

Sitting high up in a tree.

It is nighttime. She's awake.

And she is staring right at **/J/ /o/ /n/.**

Additional verses: Replace the bolded name with different student names to continue the song. For example, *And she is staring right at* **/T/ /i/ /m/.** Then, have students look at that child. For a greater challenge, invite the student whose name was given to separate the sounds of the next student's name and have the class look at that child.

Talk with the Animals

(sing to the tune of "Looby Loo")

The animals like to talk

In their own special way.

The animals like to talk.

What does the **turkey** say?

Here we go **t**ooby, **t**oo.

Here we go **t**ooby, **t**ay.

Here we go **t**ooby, **t**oo.

Now, what would the **chipmunk** say?

Here we go **ch**ooby, **ch**oo.

Here we go **ch**ooby, **ch**ay.

Here we go **ch**ooby, **ch**oo.

Now, what would the **moose** say?

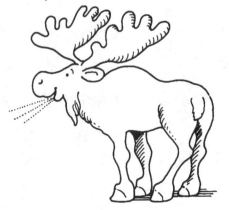

Here we go **m**ooby, **m**oo.

Here we go **m**ooby, **m**ay.

Here we go **m**ooby, **m**oo.

It's fun to talk this way.

Additional verses: Replace bolded words with other animals and replace
the bolded sounds with the initial sound in the animal's name. For example,
Now, what would the **woodpecker** *say? Here we go wooby, woo.*

♫ Funny Fall Animals ♫

(sing to the tune of "Zip-a-Dee-Doo-Dah")

Zip-a-dee-doo-dah, zip-a-dee-ay.
Oh, my, my. What a funny fall day.
Zip-a-dee-doo-dah, zip-a-dee-ay.
Turkeys sing in a different way!

Tip-a-**t**ee-**t**oo-**t**ah, **t**ip-a-**t**ee-**t**ay.
Oh, my my. What a funny fall day.
Tip-a-**t**ee-**t**oo-**t**ah, **t**ip-a-**t**ee-**t**ay.
Moose sing in a funny way!

Mip-a-**m**ee-**m**oo-**m**ah, **m**ip-a-**m**ee-**m**ay.
Oh, my my. What a funny fall day.
Mip-a-**m**ee-**m**oo-**m**ah, **m**ip-a-**m**ee-**m**ay.
Chipmunks sing in a funny way!

Chip-a-**ch**ee-**ch**oo-**ch**ah, **ch**ip-a-**ch**ee-**ch**ay.
Oh, my my. What a funny fall day.
Chip-a-**ch**ee-**ch**oo-**ch**ah, **ch**ip-a-**ch**ee-**ch**ay.
Animals sing in a funny way!

Additional verses: Replace the bolded words and sounds to continue the song.
For example, *Bears sing in a funny way!* Bip-a-bee-boo-bah, bip-a-bee-bay.

Fall Phonemic Awareness Songs & Rhymes © 1998 Creative Teaching Press

Colored Leaves

(sing to the tune of "Six Little Ducks")

So many leaves are falling on the ground.

Orange ones, yellow ones, and even brown.

But the one little leaf that rhymes with **bean**

Is my favorite color. It's the color **green.**

So many leaves are falling on the ground.

Orange ones, yellow ones, and even brown.

But the one little leaf that rhymes with **fellow**

Is my favorite color. It's the color **yellow.**

So many leaves are falling on the ground.

Orange ones, yellow ones, and even brown.

But the one little leaf that rhymes with **bed**

Is my favorite color. It's the color **red.**

Additional verses: Replace bolded words with other colors and words that rhyme with colors. For example, *But the one little leaf that rhymes with* **chew** *is my favorite color. It's the color* **blue.**

Silly Sally Squirrel

(sing to the tune of "Alouette")

Silly Sally Squirrel,

Sitting in the sun,

Singing lots of Ss until the day is done.

She sings about **soup, sun,** and **sky.**

Can you think of more? Let's try.

Additional verses: Invite students to say other words that begin with /s/ before repeating the song. Then replace the bolded words with other words that begin with /s/. For example, *She sings about **sink, skate,** and **spy.***

Fall Phonemic Awareness Songs & Rhymes © 1998 Creative Teaching Press

Owl Puppet

Phoneme Blending, Phoneme Segmentation

Have each student color, cut out, and glue to a paper lunch sack a photocopy of the Baby Owl reproducible to make an owl puppet. Ask students to sit in a circle with their baby owl puppets. While the class sings "I Saw an Owl," have students segment the sounds, blend a student's name, and turn their puppet to "stare" at that child. Continue singing the song with other students' names.

(Use with "I Saw an Owl," page 72)

Materials

- "I Saw an Owl" song (page 72)
- Baby Owl reproducible (page 93)
- crayons or markers
- scissors
- glue
- paper lunch sacks

Nocturnal Critters

Phoneme Blending

Create a chart with the headings *Who, Doing What,* and *Where.* Sing "I Saw an Owl" with the class. Ask students what other animals are awake at night. List them on the chart under the heading *Who.* Ask students what each animal does and list responses under the heading *Doing What.* Then have students decide where the animal lives and list it under *Where.* For example, *owl, sitting, tree; bat, hanging, cave; bug, flying, sky.* Invite students to sing the song, replacing the owl with the new critters. For example, *I saw a **bat**, a baby **bat** **hanging** high up in a **cave**. It is nighttime. She's awake. And she is staring right at /J/ /o/ /d/ /ee/.* Have students blend the name as they sing. Invite students to illustrate the different critters. Then, add text to the pages and bind them into a class book.

(Use with "I Saw an Owl," page 72)

Who	Doing What	Where
bat	hanging	in a cave
bug	flying	in the sky
opossum	walking	on a fence

Materials

- "I Saw an Owl" song (page 72)
- chart paper
- crayons or markers
- bookbinding materials

Animal Puppets
Phoneme Substitution

Materials

- "Talk with the Animals" song (page 73)

- construction paper

- crayons or markers

- scissors

- craft sticks

- glue

Invite students to draw a picture on construction paper of their favorite animal and cut it out. Have each student glue his or her illustration to a craft stick to make a puppet. Ask student volunteers to stand in front of the class with their puppet, and have the class sing "Talk with the Animals," substituting the names of the students' animals.

(Use with "Talk with the Animals," page 73.)

Animal Antics
Phoneme Substitution

Materials

- "Funny Fall Animals" song (page 74)

Divide the class into small groups. Ask each group to choose an animal from the "Funny Fall Animals" song to pretend to become. As the class sings the song, invite each "animal" group to come in front of the class and sing the song in its own special way. For even more fun, invite students to dramatize their animals as they sing.

(Use with "Funny Fall Animals," page 74)

Leaf Play
Rhyming

Cut out leaf shapes in several colors. Distribute one cutout to each student. Sing "Colored Leaves" with your class. Ask students to hold up their leaf when you say a word that rhymes with its color. For a greater challenge, invite student volunteers to say a word that rhymes with a color, and have the class respond by holding up the rhyming leaf color.

(Use with "Colored Leaves," page 75)

Materials

- "Colored Leaves" song (page 75)
- leaf cutouts in various colors

The Hungry Squirrel
Sound Matching

Invite each student to color, cut out, and glue to a paper lunch sack a photocopy of the Squirrel reproducible. Help students make a slit for the mouth so "food" slips in. Invite students to cut out food pictures from magazines. Tell students that Sally Squirrel can only eat foods that begin with /s/. Have students say the name of each food and "feed" it to Sally if it begins with /s/. (Have students place the remaining food pictures in a pile.)

(Use with "Silly Sally Squirrel," page 76)

Materials

- Squirrel reproducible (page 94)
- crayons or markers
- scissors
- glue
- paper lunch sacks
- magazines

Schoolhouse

Soup Bowl

In _____'s silly soup,

there are ⬜,

⬜, and ⬜.

Fall Phonemic Awareness Songs & Rhymes © 1998 Creative Teaching Press

Boy/Girl

Fall Phonemic Awareness Songs & Rhymes © 1998 Creative Teaching Press

Spinner

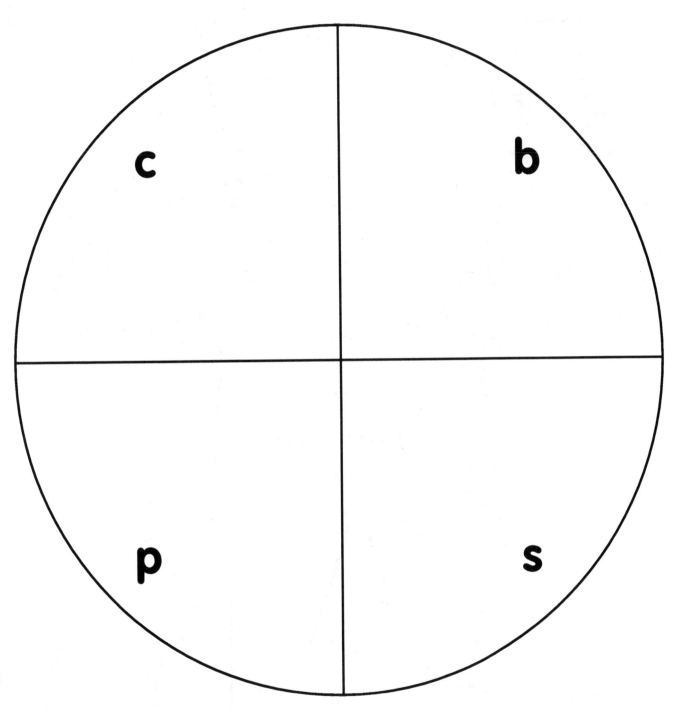

Back-to-School Picture Cards

Fall Phonemic Awareness Songs & Rhymes © 1998 Creative Teaching Press

Wheelbarrow

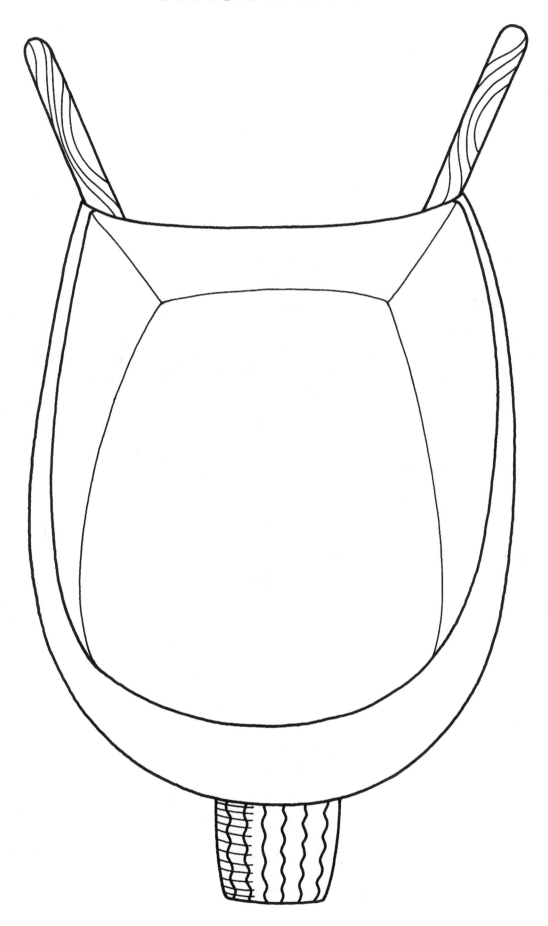

Fall Phonemic Awareness Songs & Rhymes © 1998 Creative Teaching Press

Worm Picture Cards

Fall Phonemic Awareness Songs & Rhymes © 1998 Creative Teaching Press

Apple Picture Cards

Tick-Tock Clock

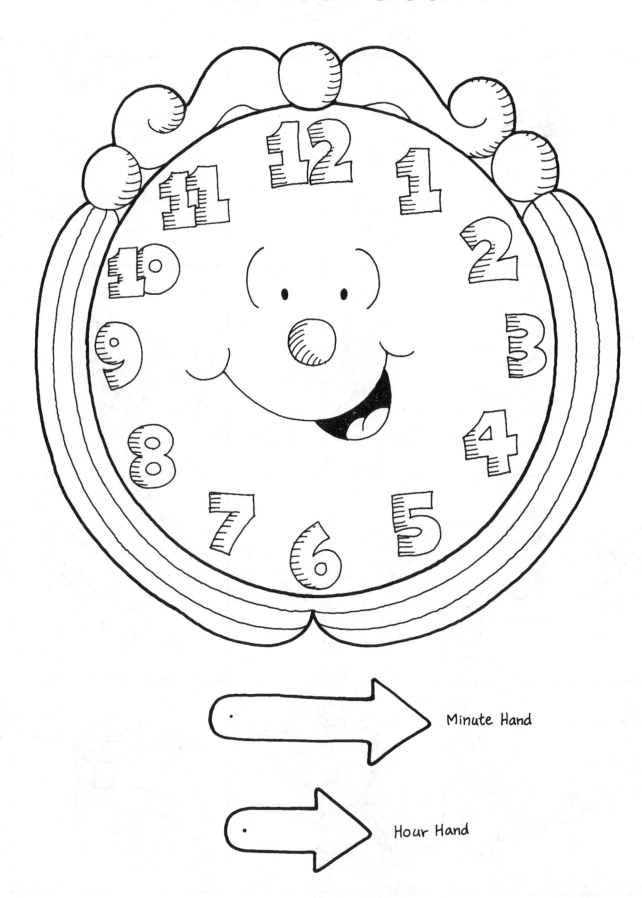

Minute Hand

Hour Hand

Fall Phonemic Awareness Songs & Rhymes © 1998 Creative Teaching Press

Counting Picture Cards

Halloween Picture Cards

Fall Phonemic Awareness Songs & Rhymes © 1998 Creative Teaching Press

Bat

Mr. Turkey

Fall Phonemic Awareness Songs & Rhymes © 1998 Creative Teaching Press

Baby Owl

Squirrel

Fall Phonemic Awareness Songs & Rhymes © 1998 Creative Teaching Press

Phonemic-Awareness Index

♫ *Song Title*